All Rights Reserved ©2019 LDH Enterprise, LLC. First Printing: 2019. The editorial arrangement, analysis, and professional commentary are subject to this copyright notice. No portion of this book may be copied, retransmitted, reposted, duplicated, or otherwise used without the express written approval of the author, except by reviewers who may quote brief excerpts in connection with a review.

United States laws and regulations are public domain and not subject to copyright. Any unauthorized copying, reproduction, translation, or distribution of any part of this material without permission by the author is prohibited and against the law.

Future Mrs.

_____

A special wedding journal for:
Thoughts
Ideas
To-Do Lists
Reminders
Notes
Checklists
Random Stuff

Made in the USA
Middletown, DE
07 July 2019